The **WAGs**
Little Book of Football

GW00656645

𝖆𝖗
RAVETTE PUBLISHING

ISBN: 978-1-84161-270-6

This edition first published in 2007 by
Ravette Publishing Limited
Unit 3, Tristar Centre, Star Road,
Partridge Green, West Sussex RH13 8RA
United Kingdom

Written by Gordon Volke

INTRODUCTION

The Beautiful Game - Yeah, Right!

Are you a footie WAG (a footballer's wife or girlfriend who stands shivering on the touchline every Saturday afternoon)?

Are you a footie-fan's WAG (the weary wife or penniless girlfriend of a fanatical supporter who follows his club *everywhere*)?

Are you a footie-watcher's WAG (wife or girlfriend of a soccer-mad couch potato who watches every single match on the telly, including foreign ones)?

If so, this book's for you!

These guys are not going to change, are they? So the answer is to beat them at their own beautiful game.

The WAGs Little Book of Football is designed to help you gen up on your other half's obsession. In a waggish and user-friendly way, it'll explain what the hell is happening out there on the pitch and why it is so important. It could change your relationship! He'll start to see you with new eyes!

Imagine the scene - a goal has just been disallowed during an England international. You yell:

"Rooney wasn't offside, ref. The full-back played him on!"

Footie-Man's eyes open wide in amazement and his jaw drops. Then he slides to the floor and stays there, staring at you. Finally, abandoning the match, he takes you in his arms and sweeps you upstairs.

Wouldn't it be worth it?

... only you know the answer to that!

In addition to the Offside Rule (which nobody really understands), you'll learn about such mysteries as the laws of the game and various positions on the pitch.

Then there's the jargon. What's that all about? All will be revealed!

Finally, there's the low-down on the various competitions, info on famous names past and present and some witty observations you can quote ... amongst a host of other things.

Can you afford to miss all this?

A Serious Business

"Some people think football is a matter of life and death," said Liverpool manager, Bill Shankly. *"I can assure them it is much more serious than that."*

So what's the big deal? What's going on out there on that hallowed turf?

The basics of the game can best be summed up in every footballer's credo -

If it's round, kick it.
If it whistles, ignore it.
If it moves, chop it down.

Football is played by two teams of 11 players on a pitch that is between 90 - 120 metres long and 45 - 90 metres wide. The idea of the game is to kick the football into the opposition's goal. The team that scores the most goals is the winner.

So far, so good.

But it's not quite as simple as that. These teams are not just collections of individuals playing a game. They are *tribes*. And the match against another team, especially a close neighbour, is a battle in a long-running *tribal war*.

So you've got to take this seriously. If you come out with the oft-quoted line: "I can't see the attraction of football. It's just 22 silly people kicking a lump of leather around a pitch," you risk alienating the members of the tribe for the rest of recorded time. You've got to understand them. This *is* more important than life or death.

Here are some vital things you need to know to follow the match/battle:

* A game lasts for 90 minutes, played in two halves of 45. A few minutes of *injury time* are added after each half.

* Sometimes, 30 minutes *extra time* is played if the match ends in a draw. This can be a terrible drag because the game was boring enough already.

* If the match is still drawn after two hours, it may be decided by a *penalty shoot-out*. These can be very exciting, but are always said to be unfair - usually by the team that loses.

*   The little man with the whistle is the *referee*. Unlike in rugby, where authority is still treated with respect, a footie ref is a figure of fun. Feel free to abuse him liberally.

*   The ref has two assistants (old name *linesmen*) who run up and down the sidelines. They are blind, slow to react and should be treated as buffoons.

*   There is also a mysterious *fourth official*, but nobody quite knows what he does, including himself.

The most important part of any match is the half time interval because:-

1. The players eat oranges, a vital step towards their 5-a-day.

2. The spectators go to the loo/ get a drink (in either order, depending on the queues).

3. The manager gets a chance to rant and rave at his players. Sadly, these team talks are confidential. They could contain useful insight into motivating your man to wash up, make the beds etc.

Who's Who And Who's Doing What?

Any self-respecting WAG needs to understand the different positions within the team...

Goalkeeper

Qualities required: reliable, brave, safe

This position is easy to spot because the goalie wears a different jersey and he is allowed to handle the ball. They say you need to be mad to play in goal, but the opposite is nearer the truth. You often do nothing for most of the game.

Full Backs

Qualities required: dedication, workhorse ethic

There are two of these, one either side of the pitch. Their main job is to stop the ball being kicked towards their goal. (Nothing funny to say about full backs. It's not a funny position.)

Centre Backs

Qualities required: Anticipation, responsible

Two of these also, in centre of field, stopping ball being kicked or headed *into* their goal. They are tough characters who look innocent as they maim the opposition

The goalkeeper, full backs and centre backs together make up the defence.

Now here's the low-down of the attack...

Midfielders

Qualities required: good vision and passing

Ah! We're in the realm of the Gods! People like Joe Cole, David Beckham, Frank Lampard and Steven Gerrard play in midfield. They control the game with their clever passes and score spectacular goals. These two positions command respect! Please remember that in all future references to midfield.

Wingers

Qualities required: fast, skillful

These guys race up and down the sides of the pitch, trying to kick the ball towards the opposition's goal. If they are right-footed, they play on the right wing. If they are left-footed, they play on the left wing. Nowadays, there seems to be a terrible shortage of left-footed players, so right-footers have to play on the left-hand side. They tend to fall over a lot.

Strikers

Qualities required: sharpness, coolness

Strikers are the superstars of the team. It's their job to score goals and, when they are successful, they rapidly become heroes. You will hear phrases like *first to react*, *clinical finishing* and *poacher* applied to strikers who score lots of goals. Phrases like *donkey*, *overpaid idiot* and **!^** *!!!*--- !!**@*! come the way of those who don't. Strikers get hugged and kissed a great deal when they score.

Teams arrange their players into formations. So if you hear phrases like *four-four-two*, *four-two-four* or *four-five-one*, that's the pattern that's been chosen.

There is always endless discussion about the relative pros and cons of these different formations. Ignore it all. It's very tedious.

The best formation ever announced was by an elderly junior school headmaster who was asked by an enthusiastic parent what formation his team played.

"Ten and one," he replied. *"One ball and ten boys trying to kick it."*

Interlude

Okay so far?

Let's take a quick break before we tackle the rules of the game.

Here are a couple of funny football stories. If you can quote them, you'll increase your footie-WAGs-cred enormously!

Newcastle United have not won anything for years. So when their manager, Glenn Roeder, suggested an all-expenses trip to Florida, his team declined. They said they'd prefer to go to Blackpool to find out what it feels like to ride on an open-top bus.

This one concerns Sebastian Coe who was invited to watch a game at Manchester United.

He arrived at the wrong gate and was prevented from getting in by a steward who told him that the VIP entrance was round the other side of the stadium.
"Do you know who I am?" cried the visitor. "I'm Sebastian Coe, the champion Olympic sprinter."
"It won't take you long to get round there then," said the steward.

Bend 'em (and Break 'em) Like Beckham

Rules, they say, are made to be broken. Nobody knows this better than footballers who try to con the ref every minute of the game and howl with outrage when the opposition does the same.

In order to appreciate their finely-honed devious skills, you need to know the rules they are breaking. Here are the important ones.

(And if you want to know more, you're fast becoming a footie-anorak!)

Colour Clash

The two teams must be easy to tell apart.
If they normally wear the same coloured
shirts, the visiting team must change into
a different colour. This is known as their
away kit - it is also a marketing man's
dream as they can sell twice the amount
of replica shirts.

Complete Tossers

At the beginning of a match, a coin is
tossed. The winner chooses whether to
kick off or choose ends.

It's All Kicking Off

One team kicks off at the start of a match, the other after half-time. Also, when a goal is scored, the team that conceded it, restarts the game by kicking off at the centre.

Corner Or Goal Kick?

When the ball goes off the end of the pitch, play is restarted in one of two ways – a corner or goal kick. If a defender put the ball out, the attacking team kicks the ball back in from a corner of the pitch. If an attacker put the ball out, the defending goalie hoofs the ball up-field and back into play.

Our Throw, Ref!

When the ball goes off the side of the pitch, it is thrown back into play in a curious, over-the-head fashion. As you'd expect, the throw goes to the team who did not put the ball out. Even though this is crystal clear, the players always appeal for the throw, even then they *know* it's the other team's.

We Was Robbed!

At either end of the pitch, in front of the goals, there is a big area called *the penalty box*. If the defending team commits a foul inside this box, it results in a *penalty* for the attacking team. This is a free kick at the goal with only the goalie to beat. Gaining a penalty is tantamount to being given a goal - unless you are an England player during the last World Cup when you couldn't score a goal for love nor money.

Red And Yellow (but not Pink and Blue)

First bad foul - you're shown a *yellow card* as a warning. Second foul in the same game - you're shown a *red card* and sent off.

OR

Really dangerous first foul - straight red card and sent off immediately.

(When a player is sent off, a substitute cannot be put on in his place. So the team has to play with 10 men ... which usually spurs them on and they win the game.)

Jargon Basement

"What the f***ing hell are they talking about?" is the question addressed in this next section.

Stand by to be let into the mysteries of football talk!

The following twenty pages contain most of the important words or phrases that you're likely to hear in connection with our National Game. And they're all arranged in alphabetical order, so you can quickly look up something you don't know.

Then try using them yourself.

Bender

Off the pitch, this is what the players go on every Saturday night after a match. On the field, it means kicking the ball in a certain way so that it flies through the air in a curve. Goals can be scored from free kicks using this technique and players who can do it are seen as very skillful and highly rated.

Building A Wall

When a free kick is awarded, the defending team can block it by putting several players in a line ten yards from the ball. This is every defender's favourite part of the game because it means you get to clutch your private parts very tightly on the pretext of preventing them from being hit by the ball.

Direct or Indirect

These terms refer to free kicks. A direct free kick can be booted straight into the opposition's goal. An indirect free kick has to touch another player first (someone on the same team as the person taking the kick.) Nobody has the foggiest idea what constitutes a direct free kick as opposed to an indirect one, even the ref. You just have to hope for a direct one because they're easier for everyone to understand.

Diving

This is the best method you can find for cheating. Imagine you're a striker, heading into the penalty box towards the opposition's goal. There are too many beefy defenders in the way to give you any hope of scoring, so you throw yourself to the ground with a cry of pain and rage to make it look like you've been fouled. With a bit of luck, the referee won't be near enough to see properly and will give a penalty. Then you make a miraculous recovery, score from the penalty spot and become the hero of the hour.

Dugout

At one side of the pitch, near the tunnel, there are two little huts or shelters, one assigned to the home team and the other to the visitors. The manager and his assistants are supposed to sit in these dugouts to watch the game, but they rarely do. They leap about in the marked-out box in front of the dugouts (*see Technical Area*).

Foul Throw

To take a throw-in properly, the ball must be held in two hands behind the head and both feet must remain on the ground throughout. Any variation on this is not allowed and results in the throw being given to the opposing team. Most ten-year-olds have mastered the art, but many fully-grown professionals playing at the highest level still get it wrong.

Goal Celebrations

Fifty years ago, a striker who scored the winning goal just got a smile or a pat on the back as he trotted back to the centre circle. Nowadays, goalscorers are buried by every member of their team leaping on top of them and crushing them to death. Recently, there's been a further fad for performing little mimes or dances that the players have agreed beforehand. These get shown on *They Think It's All Over* and the inane meaning of these antics get explained.

Handball

(*Please note* – the 'd' is never pronounced in footballing circles. You will only be considered a proper footie WAG if you say 'han-ball'.)

As you know, nobody's allowed to touch the ball except the two goalkeepers. If a player deliberately handles the ball on the pitch, it results in a direct free kick being given against him. If he commits this crime inside the penalty box, it's a penalty for the opposition. Sometimes, the ball hits a player's hand during the run of the game. Then it's up to the referee to decide whether it was an accident or deliberate handball. What the ref decides depends on what mood he's in or which side he's on.

High Tackle

Shame on you! This has nothing to do with a nine-foot-tall footballer wearing tight shorts. It's a dangerous type of tackle, sometimes called *foot up*, where one player raises his foot too high and can knock out or seriously injure the person he is tackling.

Hitting The Bar

This does not mean going for a drink, though that could be a sensible option on a freezing cold afternoon when the score remains nil-nil. The bar in question is the crossbar and hitting it means being tantalisingly close to getting a goal.

In The Box

Unlike cricket, where the box and what's in it means something entirely different, the footie box is a shorthand name for the penalty area. Getting the ball in the box means you're likely to score a goal or have one scored against you.

Markers and Marking

If you're told to mark a player, you follow him everywhere round the pitch and make sure you get in his way, give him the occasional kick and generally stop him from playing. If he's clever, he'll give you the slip (known as *losing your marker*) and shame you by scoring a goal.

Nutmeg

This strange phrase means to pass the ball through an opponent's legs. This being football, it should be quite obvious where the nuts come into it. To be nutmegged is regarded as a considerable insult and you're a smart cookie if you can get away with it.

Own Goal

Where would the compilers of funny
football DVDs be without own goals –
players accidentally kicking the ball into
their own net and scoring for the
opposition? It is the ultimate shame and
you're allowed to feel motherly when
you see the unfortunate defender
hanging his head or sobbing quietly as
his team mates glare flaming daggers of
hate at him.

Route 1

Attacking the opposition's goal by going straight up the middle of the pitch, a simple and direct approach. A big boot from the goalie or a centre back is often how this move starts. The phrase could also apply to the lovemaking technique favoured by teenage footballers (and also by many grown-up ones if they're really honest).

Scissor Kick

This is a flashy move in which a player launches himself into the air and tries to kick the ball backwards over his head. Usually, he just goes arse over tit and the ball flies over the roof of the stand. But to score with a scissor kick is very spectacular and, if you pull it off, you gain god-like status immediately.

Selling A Dummy

This means swerving aside to fool a defender, allowing the ball to run on to one of your team mates. It has nothing to do with putting an overpaid, under-achieving player on the transfer list.

Short Corner

Most corner kicks are booted straight towards the opposition's goal. Sometimes, however, the ball is just passed to another player standing nearby. This is called taking a *short corner* or *taking it short* (not to be confused with *getting caught short*). The idea is to take the defence by surprise, but usually it doesn't work and the whole business can be a bit of a waste of time.

Six Yard Box

The little area right in front of each goal. It has no real purpose other than showing where to put the ball for a goal kick.

Spitting

There is a huge double-standard regarding this practice. It's perfectly okay for players to gob enormous greenies onto the pitch in the name of clearing their airways. Indeed, it's become an art form in the way you blow your chunk and make it arc gracefully to the ground. However, if you spit at another player, you're a disgusting, filthy animal and deserve to be castrated.

Square Ball

And that would be very hard to play with! No, the phrase means a particular type of pass – across the field, from one side to the other, without the ball going forward.

Step-overs

Fast, tricky players like wingers like to fool defenders by stepping over the ball, making their opponent go the wrong way. It's a smart move, but some players do it too often and make several step-overs, one after the other. Then they look like drunks whose legs are out of control and they often lose the ball, having totally bamboozled themselves.

Technical Area

There is nothing remotely technical about this area. It is a little marked-out pen in front of the dugouts where the managers of each team pace about like caged lions, roaring instructions that the players don't hear or choose to ignore. (Actually, thinking about it, there is definitely something *very* technical about the swearwords used by each manager, many combinations of which have never been heard before.)

The Tunnel

As the two teams leave their dressing rooms, they walk up the tunnel and out onto the pitch. Usually, the opposing sides joke together and hold the hands of little children who look a) terrified, b) bursting to go to the toilet, or c) both. At half time or after the game, however, this tunnel often becomes a violent battleground where disgruntled players who have been fouled or insulted, punch each other's lights out in the forlorn hope that nobody can see what they're doing.

Footie Funnies

Time for another quick break before we stray offside...

Name three football clubs whose names contain swear words.
Arsenal, Scunthorpe and f*****g Chelsea!

What tea do soccer players drink?
PenalTea!

What's the difference between a Scottish football fan and a coconut?
You can get a drink out of a coconut

Why do Newcastle fans plant potatoes round the sides of St James Park?

So they have something to lift at the end of the season.

And supposing these football teams were women...

Birmingham City / Britney Spears

Has been threatening to go down for the last few years, but finally did it recently.

West Ham / Barbara Windsor

We've been laughing at those tits for so long, we've forgotten that at one time they looked quite good.

Charlton / Tara Palmer-Tompkinson

Looks quite good at the back, but nothing much to speak of up front.

The Biggie

This is what you've been waiting for. The big one. The Offside Rule!

Understand this and you'll be three-quarters of the way to becoming a fully-qualified footie WAG, welcomed by men and women of the footballing fraternity anywhere in the world.

And, believe it or not, it isn't really that difficult. All the hoo-haa surrounding it comes from the problems of applying the rule during the game. Split-second decisions made by the officials can win or lose vital matches.

First of all, it helps to understand why there is an Offside Rule in the first place.

Well, without it, the strikers would be able to hang around right in front of their opposition's goal. The ball could be passed to them all the time and they would keep scoring. So the match would end up like a kid's game in the playground and the final scores would be 21-17 or more.

With the Offside Rule in place, this doesn't happen. So what does it state? Here it is in its simplest form...

An attacking player is in an offside position if, when the ball is passed to him by a team-mate, he does not have two opposing players between him and the goal.

One of these opposing players is usually the goalie. So, in reality, the striker must have at least one defender in front of him to remain on side.

* If a striker strays offside (ie. approaches the opposition's goal without two defenders in front of him), the linesman raises his flag and play stops.

* Goals scored from an offside position do not count.

* Play is restarted by the defending team taking an indirect free kick.

So far, so good? But it's not quite as simple as that! (Would you expect anything different?) There has been a recent addition to the rule that totally muddies the water!

A couple of years ago, an amendment was introduced that says a player *can* remain in an Offside Position provided he is:

"Not actively involved in play."

In other words, if a striker strays offside but isn't where the ball is, he's okay.

This has caused no end of confusion because it's often impossible to decide whether someone is involved in the play or not. So don't worry too much about this bit. Nobody else has got a clue, either.

Okay to keep going? We're nearly there!

Here are some additional bits to remember about everyone's favourite footie rule...

1. *You cannot be offside in your own half of the pitch.*

2. *You're not offside if you're right in front of goal and the ball comes to you directly from a goal kick, throw-in, or corner.*

3. *You're not offside if you are level with the last two defenders.*

Got it now?
Or are you losing the will to live?

Obviously, with a rule like this, teams can use it to their own advantage. How? By playing what's called *The Offside Trap*.

Imagine you're a defender for Rovers and United are coming at you with an attack. "Right, lads," you shout to the other defenders either side of you. "Out!" Then you all charge up the field together in a line, leaving United's attackers all stranded in offside positions. The linesman flags like mad, PHEEP goes the ref's whistle and your team gets a free kick, having completely smashed up United's attack.

Clever stuff, eh? Except that it doesn't always work! It only needs bad timing or a dozy linesman and the attackers get through, gaining an easy chance on goal. This is called *beating* or *springing the offside trap*.

Final Thought

The *real* purpose of the Offside Rule is to create controversy. Without it, the managers would have nothing to rage about, the pundits on telly would have nothing to talk about and the pub would be silent.

Winner Wonderland

Have you heard of the *Championship*?
What's the difference between the *FA
Cup* and the *League Cup*? Who plays in
the *Champions League* and the *World Cup*?

Questions like these are apt to baffle a
rookie football WAG. There's such a
bewildering array of Leagues and Cups
that it's impossible to tell who's
competing in what.

Once again, however, help is at hand.
Stand by for the WAG's Potted Guide to
all the major footie competitions.

The Premiership

Top English league manned almost exclusively by overseas players. Contains all the big clubs like *Chelsea*, *Manchester United* and *Arsenal*. All the matches are televised worldwide and watched by zillions of people.

The Championship

The league below. Everyone wants to get into the Premiership because there's loads more money there. Only three teams go up at the end of each season as the bottom three clubs from the Premiership are relegated.

League One

Basically, division three!

League Two

Don't bother about this league unless your local team is in it.

The Conference

The league just below the four leagues in the FA (Football Association.) Small grounds, small crowds and loads of passion.

The FA Cup

This is a knockout competition featuring all 92 clubs in the four divisions of the FA. Can be exciting when little teams from the lower leagues get drawn to play the big boys. The Final is a big occasion held in May.

The League Cup

Another knockout competition. Often named after its sponsors, eg. *The Milk Cup*, The *Coca-Cola Cup*. Seen by some as one competition too many these days.

The Charity Shield

A one-off match between the winners of last year's Premiership and FA Cup. Staged in August as a curtain-raiser for the new season.

The Champions League

These are those mid-week games that interfere with *Eastenders* and *Coronation Street*. It's a competition for all the clubs in Europe that come top of their Premier leagues the previous season.
Can be interesting when English teams get to the latter stages, but it's often a long, boring old slog on the way.

The UEFA Cup

Another European competition, a sort of poor-man's Champions League.

The World Cup

This is the big one, the ultimate prize in football. Staged every four years. Not a club competition. This is *international* football between teams from different countries around the world. Very big business. The host nation usually does well.

The European Championships

Often shortened to Euro and the year it's taking place eg. Euro 2008. Also played every four years. Alternates with the World Cup, so one or the other comes up every two years. Only countries in Europe (and surrounding area) take part in this one.

Qualifiers

Only the winners of the last World Cup or the European Championship automatically go in the draw for the next competition. Everyone else has to play a series of qualifying matches and gain enough points to get to the finals. These qualifiers can be very exciting or deeply disappointing depending on the fate of your national team.

Friendly Internationals

Avoid these at all costs. Friendly matches between different countries are practice games in which the managers try out different players. They serve no purpose beyond this, so they're pretty tedious to watch. The only excitement comes if the game turns out to be an 'unfriendly' and the teams start to care who wins.

Testimonial Matches

These are never televised, so you won't see one unless you go along to the ground. They're held to reward and honour players who have given long-standing service to their club. The money from the game goes to the player concerned (not that they need it much nowadays) and generally it's an emotional, heart-warming sort of affair.

Reserve Matches

All the big football clubs run at least one
reserve team. Their purpose is to keep
players not in the first team out of
mischief and give star players recovering
from injury somewhere to get match fit.
Never televised and not watched by very
many people. Not important, even to a
budding footie-WAG like you.

Play-Offs

These matches can be very exciting,
especially if you support one of the
teams involved. They are staged near the
end of every season to decide the final
promotion places. The teams that came

first and second in the Championship, League One and League Two all go up automatically, but the teams that finish third, fourth, fifth and sixth go into this mini knockout competition within each league. The respective winners gain the third promotion place to the next division.

The Inter-Toto Cup

This is some strange, extra club competition that English teams occasionally enter.

Pre-Season Friendlies and Tours

Most of the big clubs play a few friendly matches with British or overseas teams towards the end of the off-season break in July and August. The idea is to hit the ground running when the season proper starts. Like international friendlies, they are of no interest to anyone whatsoever other than fanatical followers of the clubs concerned.

It Don't Arf Hurt, Mum!

Another area of must-understand footie jargon concerns common injuries to the players. These are the ones you need to know...

Hamstring

This is the big thigh muscle that footballers are forever pulling or straining. It stops them running or kicking and they're usually out of the game for two or three weeks.

Metatarsals

These are the bones that link the toes to the foot. Until David Beckham and Wayne Rooney broke them just before important international competitions, nobody except doctors had ever heard of them. The whisper is that these toe injuries are caused by the flashy, slipper-like boots that the top players wear these days. If they borrowed a pair from Stanley Matthews (a superstar of the Fifties who wore boots like clodhoppers smothered in dubbin) they wouldn't get these problems.

Groin Strains

Another oft-quoted ailment. The question here is – how exactly did they strain their groins in the first place?

Clash of Heads

OUCH! The most painful and dangerous of football injuries. You're entitled to feel concerned when both players go down clutching their heads and spurting blood everywhere. (Famously, in the Eighties, Terry Butcher played a whole match for England with a badly bleeding head wound, an act of bravery that has never been forgotten.) Nowadays, the sight of any blood means that the player must leave the field for treatment.

Heading The Ball

Some people argue that heading the ball is bad for your brain. The constant violent blows to the head upset the brain's stability and this leads to memory loss in later life. Still, this doesn't seem to stop anyone becoming a professional footballer. With wages at £150,000 a week, or whatever, who cares?

A Quota Of Quotes

Here's some footie wit and wisdom for you to enjoy (and maybe remember if you haven't been doing too much heading lately!).

Football's a funny old game.
Jimmy Greaves

We deserved to win this game after hammering them 0 – 0 in the first half.
Kevin Keegan

I never comment on referees and I'm not going to break the habit of a lifetime for that prat!
Ron Atkinson

And I honestly believe we can go all the way to Wembley ... unless somebody knocks us out.
Dave Bassett

More football later, but first let's see the goals from the Scottish Cup Final.
Des Lynam

I never make predictions and I never will.
Paul Gascoigne

Newcastle, of course, are unbeaten in their last five wins.
Brian Moore

If history is going to repeat itself, I think we should expect the same thing again.
Terry Venables

For those of you watching in black and white, Spurs are in the all-yellow strip.
John Motson

What will you do when you leave football, Jack? Will you stay in football?
Stuart Hall

That's football, Mike. Northern Ireland have had several chances and haven't scored, but England have had no chances and have scored twice.
Trevor Brooking

There's no way Ryan Giggs is another George Best. He's another Ryan Giggs.
Dennis Law

I can see the carrot at the end of the tunnel.
Stuart Pearce

And with 4 minutes gone, the score is already 0-0.
Ian Dark

The first 90 minutes are the most important.
Bobby Robson

Viv Anderson has pissed a fatness test.
John Helm

Aston Villa are seventh in the league. That's almost as high as you can get without being in the top six.
Ian Payne

He's signalling to the bench with his groin.
Mark Bright

Names Of The Game

If you attain the status of a fully qualified footie-WAG and start moving in footballing circles, you'll be expected to know the names of certain people and places and their relative importance.

So here's the cheat...

Wembley
Our national stadium. Currently being rebuilt. Should be an exciting venue if it ever gets finished.

The Millennium Stadium
In Cardiff. Standing in for Wembley until it's ready. Has a posh roof that opens and closes.

Pelé

A Brazilian boy from a poor background who became a superstar in the Fifties and Sixties. Regarded as possibly the greatest player of all time. Universally respected.

Bobby Moore

Another legendary player. Captain of the England team that won the World Cup in 1966. Died of liver cancer at a tragically young age.

Old Trafford

Home ground of Manchester United (nickname The Red Devils), the team you used to love or hate because they had the most money and won everything.

Stamford Bridge

Home ground of Chelsea FC (nickname The Blues or The Pensioners), the team you now have to love or hate because they have even more money and win almost everything.

George Best

Soccer genius from Belfast whose amazing skills thrilled the world in the Sixties and Seventies and saddened it thereafter as he drank himself to death.

Geoff Hurst

The only player ever to score a hat trick in a World Cup Final (England's 4-2 victory over Germany in 1966).

Bobby Charlton
Famous for scoring the most goals for England and the wisp of hair that used to flow across his otherwise bald head.

Gary Lineker
Scored one less goal for England than Bobby Charlton. Never booked in his playing career. Now presents *Match Of The Day*.

And not forgetting...

Archie Thomson
The Australian player who scored 13 goals in his country's 31-0 defeat of Samoa in a World Cup qualifier in 2001. It's the highest individual tally and the highest overall score in an international match *ever*.

Last Laugh

Ready for a couple of well-known funny soccer stories? Good! You need to relax and stay cool before your big footie-WAG exam that's coming up next!

Dozy Dave arrives at the match half way through the second half.
"I got stuck in the traffic," he says.
"What's the score?"
"Nil-nil," replies person in the next seat.
"And what was the score at half time?" adds Dave.

Peter and Paul were working when England played Spain, so they taped the match and watched it next day.

"Bet you a fiver England win," said Paul.

"You're on," agreed Peter. "Spain's going to walk it!"

The match turned out to be a 3-0 victory to England, so Peter handed over the money.

"I can't take this," confesses Paul. "I knew the score."

"So did I," said Peter. "But I still made the bet because I didn't think Spain would lose twice."

Have you been paying attention?

Time to test your footie-WAG-ology!

Here are some quick quiz questions about the wonderful world of football. Tot up your score and then check your status against the special Score Rating.

1. What is a *NUTMEG*?

   a) A Spice
   b) A painful injury
   c) A smart footballing move

2. What nationality is *PELÉ*?

3. If a striker is passed the ball and only has the goalie to beat, is he *OFFSIDE*?

   a) Yes
   b) No
   c) Who cares?

4. *EXTRA TIME* lasts a further 45 minutes.

   a) True
   b) False

5. Whereabouts in the body is the *METATARSAL* bone?

6. If two teams wear similar coloured shirts, what happens when they play against each other?

   a) The home team has to change
   b) The away team has to change
   c) One team wears coloured bibs

7. Complete the name of the player who scored the most goals for England.

   B _ _ _ _   C _ _ _ _ _ _ _

8. What is the *CONFERENCE*?

    a) An annual meeting to discuss football
    b) A league below the 4 Football Leagues
    c) A famous pear-shaped stadium

9. What happens if you are shown a *STRAIGHT RED CARD*?

10. Can you complete Bill Shankly's famous quote about Football (or the gist of it)?

    Some people think football is a matter of life and death. I can assure them ...

11. Which team plays at *OLD TRAFFORD?*

12. How often is the WORLD CUP staged?

    a) Every year
    b) Every two years
    c) Every four years

13. What is *GEOFF HURST'S* great claim to fame?

14. What is the *TECHNICAL AREA*?

15. Which one of these is not a
    FOOTBALL FORMATION?

    a) 4-4-2
    b) 4-2-4
    c) 4-4-4

Answers

1. c) A smart footballling move
2. Pelé is Brazilian
3. a) Yes – offside!
4. b) False (It is only 30 minutes)
5. In the foot
6. b) The away team has to change
7. Bobby Charlton
8. b) A league below the 4 football leagues
9. You are sent off straight away
10. ...it is much more serious than that
11. Manchester United
12. c) Every four years
13. Only player to score a hat trick in a World Cup Final
14. Pen for the managers in front of the dugouts
15. c) 4-4-4 (That makes 12 players on the pitch, as well as the goalie, of course!)

Score Ratings

0 - 5 right:

Congratulations! You've qualified as a Footie-WAG with Third Class Honours.

6 - 10 right:

Excellent! You've scored a superb Second and are now a fully recognised Footie-WAG.

11 - 15 right:

Brilliant! You've become a First Class Footie-WAG with full honours, streamers and bells on!

Alternative

Ending

If you've had quite enough of this soccer stuff, here's an escape route that may appeal to you more!

Don't be a footie-loving WAG, be a PROPER footballer's WAG like Posh or Coleen!

Here is how to qualify -

1. Wear huge designer sunglasses.
2. Keep your fake tan well topped up.
3. Always have lots of BLING on display.
4. Know where the cameras are and have a pout ready for them at all times.

5. Never be seen without full make-up, even when popping out for the paper.
6. Use your mobile phone as often as you can.
7. Shop 'til you drop every day and make sure you're seen carrying bags from the most expensive boutiques.
8. Drive a chunky 4-wheel drive off-roader.
9. Live in a mansion.
10. Make sure you appear in *Hello* or *OK* magazines as often as possible.
11. Drink a great deal and behave badly.

12. Be seen to be drinking a great deal and behaving badly.

13. Have the occasional falling-out with your fellow WAGs.

14. Only go to the trendiest nightclubs.

15. Wear hair extensions if you can.

16. Wear designer tracksuits to look sporty.

17. Talk with a hint of an Essex accent.

18. Announce plans for a totally over-the-top wedding in the near future.

19. Pretend to like football.

20. *Hate* football.

So the final question is ... can you afford all this?